Camas Monitoring at Nez Perce National Historical Park and Big Hole National Battlefield

UPPER COLUMBIA
BASIN NETWORK

UCBN

2008 Annual Status Report

Natural Resource Technical Report NPS/UCBN/NRTR—2008/133

Thomas J. Rodhouse
National Park Service, Upper Columbia Basin Network
Central Oregon Community College, 2600 NW College Way – Ponderosa Building
Bend, OR 97701-5998

Lisa K. Garrett
National Park Service, Upper Columbia Basin Network
University of Idaho, Department of Fish and Wildlife
Moscow, ID 83844-1136

November 2008

U.S. Department of the Interior
National Park Service
Natural Resource Program Center
Fort Collins, Colorado

The Natural Resource Publication series addresses natural resource topics that are of interest and applicability to a broad readership in the National Park Service and to others in the management of natural resources, including the scientific community, the public, and the NPS conservation and environmental constituencies. Manuscripts are peer-reviewed to ensure that the information is scientifically credible, technically accurate, appropriately written for the intended audience, and is designed and published in a professional manner.

The Natural Resource Technical Report series is used to disseminate the peer-reviewed results of scientific studies in the physical, biological, and social sciences for both the advancement of science and the achievement of the National Park Service's mission. The reports provide contributors with a forum for displaying comprehensive data that are often deleted from journals because of page limitations. Current examples of such reports include the results of research that addresses natural resource management issues; natural resource inventory and monitoring activities; resource assessment reports; scientific literature reviews; and peer reviewed proceedings of technical workshops, conferences, or symposia.

Views, statements, findings, conclusions, recommendations and data in this report are solely those of the author(s) and do not necessarily reflect views and policies of the U.S. Department of the Interior, National Park Service. Mention of trade names or commercial products does not constitute endorsement or recommendation for use by the National Park Service.

Printed copies of reports in these series may be produced in a limited quantity and they are only available as long as the supply lasts. This report is also available from the Upper Columbia Basin Network and NRPM websites (http://www.nature.nps.gov/im/units/UCBN and http://www.nature.nps.gov/publications/NRPM, respectively) on the internet, or by sending a request to the address on the back cover.

Please cite this publication as:
Rodhouse, T. J., and L. K. Garrett. 2008. Camas monitoring at Nez Perce National Historical Park and Big Hole National Battlefield: 2008 Status Report. Natural Resource Technical Report NPS/UCBN/NRTR—2008/133. National Park Service, Fort Collins, Colorado.

NPS D-76, November 2008

Contents

Figures

Tables

Executive Summary

The mission of the National Park Service is "to conserve unimpaired the natural and cultural resources and values of the national park system for the enjoyment of this and future generations" (NPS 1999). To uphold this goal, the Director of the NPS approved the Natural Resource Challenge to encourage national parks to focus on the preservation of the nation's natural heritage through science, natural resource inventories, and expanded resource monitoring (NPS 1999). Through the Challenge, 270 parks in the national park system were organized into 32 inventory and monitoring networks.

The Upper Columbia Basin Network has identified 14 priority park vital signs, indicators of ecosystem health, which represent a broad suite of ecological phenomena operating across multiple temporal and spatial scales. Our intent has been to monitor a balanced and integrated "package" of vital signs that meets the needs of current park management, but will also be able to accommodate unanticipated environmental conditions in the future. Camas is one particularly high priority vital sign for two UCBN parks, Big Hole National Battlefield (BIHO) and Nez Perce National Historical Park (NEPE). Camas is a unique resource for these parks because it is both culturally and ecologically significant. Camas was and remains one of the most widely utilized indigenous foods in the Pacific Northwest and it is strongly associated with the wet prairie ecosystems of the region that have been degraded or lost due to historic land use practices. A long-term citizen science-based monitoring program for detecting status and trends in camas populations at BIHO and Weippe Prairie, a subunit of NEPE, will serve as a central information source for park adaptive management decision making and will provide essential feedback on any eventual restoration efforts of park wet prairie habitats. The involvement of student citizen scientists in this particular program has been effective both in terms of leveraging resources as well as in engaging communities in park stewardship and science education.

This annual report details the status and trend estimates obtained from the first four years of monitoring, 2005-2008, at Weippe Prairie and BIHO. Overall trends in camas density are stable to slightly increasing, although these results are preliminary and should be interpreted cautiously. Camas populations across the two park units range widely in abundance, with densities of two of the five Weippe Prairie management zones, A and D, estimated at 60 plants/m^2. BIHO and Weippe Prairie management zone E exhibited the lowest densities, at 6 plants/m^2. Historical densities were estimated to be 100 plants/m^2 or more in high-quality sites. The ratio of flowering to total established camas plants was consistently higher at BIHO than at Weippe Prairie during 2005-2008. Flowering ratio appeared to be most stable over time in zones A and D. Invasion by sulfur cinquefoil (*Potentilla recta*) and orange hawkweed (*Hieracium aurantiacum*), as measured by frequency of occurrence in quadrats, appeared to be stable or slightly declining, and was lowest overall in management zones A and D. No discernible correlations between annual precipitation and density have emerged as of yet, although this will require several more years to evaluate adequately. There is no relationship between thatch depth and camas density or flowering stem density, and we recommend that thatch depth measurements be discontinued in future sampling except in zone C in order to reduce field sampling time. This change will be reflected in a revised version of the UCBN camas monitoring protocol pending approval by park managers.

Introduction

Camas (*Camassia quamash* [Pursh] Greene) is a perennial bulb-producing lily (Family Liliaceae; alternatively Agavaceae, APG 2003) that was and remains one of the most widely utilized plant foods of the Nez Perce people (Harbinger 1964; Hunn 1981; Turner and Kuhnlein 1983; Thoms 1989; Mastrogiuseppe 2000). Camas was also a focal resource at many of the significant historical events memorialized by Big Hole National Battlefield (BIHO) and Nez Perce National Historical Park (NEPE). It was during the camas harvest at Weippe Prairie, a subunit of NEPE, where the Lewis and Clark Corps of Discovery first encountered the Nez Perce. The battle at Big Hole occurred at a traditional Nez Perce camas harvesting campsite. It is also noteworthy that the botanical "type" specimen for the *Camassia* genus as well as for *C. quamash* itself was collected by the Lewis and Clark expedition returning through the Weippe Prairie during the spring of 1806 (Meehan 1898; Gould 1942).

Camas is considered a facultative wetland species (Reed 1988) that is strongly associated with the seasonal wet prairie ecosystems of the interior Columbia Plateau which are represented at the Weippe Prairie, a subunit of NEPE, and along the North Fork of the Big Hole River, where the Big Hole Battlefield is located. Large expanses of camas in bloom were noted by numerous explorers and botanists that entered the Pacific Northwest in the 19th century, including the Lewis and Clark expedition, and which were frequently described as "blue lakes" when viewed from a distance (Havard 1895; Leiberg 1897; Murphey 1987; Thoms 1989). The extent of the wet prairie ecosystem type has been drastically reduced in the Columbia Basin as a result of agricultural conversion, irrigation and flood control development, and other land use practices (Thoms 1989; Dahl 1990; Taft and Haig 2003). Remaining wet prairies in the region are often structurally altered and compromised by non-native and woody native invasive species. The NPS-owned portions of Weippe Prairie and the Big Hole valley are no exception. Both sites have historic agricultural developments that have altered site hydrology, are impacted by invasive weeds, and Weippe Prairie has also been used for intensive haying and grazing. Orange hawkweed (*Hieracium aurantiacum*) and sulfur cinquefoil (*Potentilla recta*), listed as invasive plants in Idaho, are present at Weippe Prairie and part of the focus of current park weed management. Competition from invasive weed species, including the aforementioned forbs as well as thatch-building grasses such as timothy (*Phleum pratense*), may impact camas populations within the UCBN through competition. Reduced fire frequency has allowed black hawthorn (*Cretaegus douglasii*) to become established in the prairie, and this may eventually cause an undesirable shift in prairie plant vegetation, including a reduction in camas. Park managers at NEPE have discontinued grazing as of 2007 but still permit limited haying in portions of Weippe Prairie. Herbicide applications at Weippe Prairie, and to a lesser extent at BIHO, continue as part of the parks' integrated weed management programs. The impacts of these activities on camas populations are not well understood at this time but are potential stressors as well.

Despite the continued impacts of modern anthropogenic stressors on what appear to be markedly reduced camas populations, the wet prairies of BIHO and NEPE, like their better studied analogues in Oregon's Willamette Valley, are highly productive ecosystems that exhibit a good potential for restoration (Taft and Haig 2003). A long-term monitoring program for detecting status and trends in camas populations at BIHO and Weippe Prairie will serve as a central information source for park adaptive management decision making and will provide essential feedback on any eventual restoration efforts. Camas monitoring will be particularly important at Weippe Prairie because it is the focal resource for the site, and because the site remains actively sprayed and mowed, and is a likely target for park restoration efforts in the future. The National Park Service acquired the Weippe Prairie property in 2003 and does not yet have a developed management plan. The implementation of camas monitoring early in the process of NPS management at Weippe Prairie is timely and will greatly facilitate science-based decision making. Park management has considerable latitude in the strategies and tools employed there. At BIHO, where management is less intense and opportunities for restoration are few, given the cultural sensitivity of the battlefield, camas monitoring will still provide an invaluable indication of overall status and trend of the camas population and its supporting wetland over time.

It is hoped that the UCBN camas monitoring program will deliver timely and helpful information to park managers. Both park sites are managing to preserve the historic landscapes of which camas is a central component. Camas is a facultative wetland species that should respond conspicuously to perturbations in the wet prairie ecosystems of Weippe Praire and BIHO, thus making it an effective indicator of overall ecological condition. Restoration of the Weippe Prairie to increase camas populations is emerging as a real interest to park management and therefore makes this monitoring effort a critically important source of information for that park. Camas monitoring results can help in the development of restoration targets and in the evaluation of any eventual site manipulations. The design of the sampling frame at Weippe Prairie included the creation of 5 management zones, setting in motion quasi-experimental opportunities for the future, where management treatments might be applied to some zones, leaving other zones as controls. We have adopted the recommendations made by Bennetts et al. (2007) and begun the identification of early-warning assessment points. Our first assessment point is a 25% decline in mean camas density. A concomitant 25% increase is also an assessment point, but one better described as an initial desired condition benchmark rather than an early-warning sign (Bennetts et al. 2007). These were arrived at as starting points in the face of considerable uncertainty concerning camas synecology, were logistically and statistically feasible, and inherently conservative. We will look to add new assessment points as our knowledge about camas and the wet prairie ecosystem grows. This report is the first step in this process.

The National Park Service initiated a camas monitoring program at NEPE and BIHO in 2005, assisted in large part by student "citizen scientists" who participate in annual spring field data collection. The field effort involves counting all established camas plants within quadrats, as well as those plants that flower during that growing season. Thatch depth and the presence of target invasive weeds are also measured in each quadrat. Weather is an additional important driver of camas population dynamics, and summaries from weather stations near each of the parks will be used in modeling long-term trends.

We report here on the 2008 sampling results from both Weippe Prairie and Big Hole Battlefield, and include data from 2005-2007 to provide context for current estimates of camas density. Changes were made in design and methodology of the sampling protocol during the first three years. We have made some adjustments to the data from these early years, and with some assumptions and caveats, we can compare results from each year and begin to identify baseline patterns of density. Some interesting patterns are emerging in these data, which will serve to

2

stimulate new hypotheses and assessment points. With the protocol complete and the design and methodology stabilized, we can now begin to accumulate a robust long-term data set. Given the predictions of profound climate change in the Pacific Northwest and a considerable land use legacy, monitoring UCBN camas prairies over time is sure to shed new light on the important issues of ecosystem recovery, resistance, and resilience.

Objectives

The monitoring objectives for this program are:

- Estimate mean established plant and flowering stem densities (status) in the camas populations of Weippe Prairie and within the targeted portion of the Big Hole National Battlefield.
- Determine trends (net trend, as reviewed by MacDonald 2003) in the densities of established camas populations in Weippe Prairie and BIHO.
- Determine trends in the proportion of flowering to non-flowering camas plants in Weippe Prairie and BIHO.
- Determine trends in the frequency of occurrence of targeted invasive plants (currently these are orange hawkweed and sulfur cinquefoil).
- Determine the magnitude and direction of camas density response to measurable explanatory variables such as winter precipitation, graminoid thatch depth, and specific management activities.

Note: "Established camas plants" are those plants expressing 2 or more leaves and excludes single-leaved seedlings. The significance of this distinction is discussed in greater detail in the UCBN camas monitoring protocol (Rodhouse et al. 2007).

This report summarizes status and trend estimates for camas populations over the period 2005-2008. A more in depth trend analysis report will be presented in 2011, five years after completion of the final sampling protocol.

Methods

The UCBN initiated camas monitoring in 2005 at the Weippe Prairie, a NEPE unit, located in Weippe, Idaho. Monitoring was initiated at BIHO, located near Wisdom, Montana, in 2006. Figures 1 and 2 show the sampling frames and 2008 sampling points for each park unit.

Sampling methods followed those detailed by Rodhouse et al. (2007). Students from the Oregon Museum of Science and Industry (OMSI) and local high schools conducted the majority of field sampling, under field leadership and supervision from NPS staff. The approach is quadrat-based and involves the measurement of camas plant density, camas flowering stem density, graminoid thatch depth, and the presence of targeted invasive plant species. A systematic sample of one-hundred-seventy-seven 0.5 m^2 quadrats was measured at Weippe Prairie in 2005 and was considered a pilot effort. Management zone D in Weippe Prairie was not sampled in 2005. Weippe Prairie was completely surveyed in 2006 using a simple random sampling design with long, narrow 0.6 m^2 quadrats, and this design was used in all subsequent years at both park units. At BIHO, historical and cultural concerns led to the development of a targeted sampling frame with arbitrary boundaries that encompassed the largest and most abundant portion of the camas population in that park. Sample sizes at Weippe Prairie were 220, 283, and 360 for the years 2006-2008, respectively. At BIHO, sample sizes were 100, 124, and 150 for the same three years. All camas plants were included in camas density counts in 2005 and 2006, but a protocol change beginning in 2007 led to the exclusion of single-leaved seedlings. Camas seedlings are ephemeral and highly variable in their germination, and this led us to focus the protocol on *established* camas plants beginning in 2007. This is the most significant methodological change and one that requires careful and cautious consideration of comparisons among years.

Camas flowering stem density was measured at each quadrat beginning in 2006. Mature camas plants produce one conspicuous and persistent inflorescence each year, making flowering stem counts reliable and direct. Not all mature plants flower in a given year, however, and variability in flowering is of interest to the UCBN. Graminoid thatch depth was measured at each quadrat beginning in 2006 as well. Thatch depth was measured in three pre-established locations along the quadrat long axis and averaged. The presence or absence of two target weed species, sulfur cinquefoil and orange hawkweed, was noted in each quadrat for use in measures of frequency of occurrence at Weippe Prairie. There currently are no weed species being recorded in quadrats at BIHO, as no high priority weed species have been encountered in the sampling frame there. Precipitation data was obtained from the Remote Automated Weather Station (RAWS) in Pierce, Idaho (Station 107046) for Weippe Prairie and the cooperative weather station in Wisdom, Montana (Station 249067). These stations are located approximately 11 and 10 miles from the respective parks, and are the closest available weather stations. Data from these stations provide an approximation of regional precipitation patterns immediately preceding and during the 4-year sampling period.

Early monitoring results quickly indicated that density counts were extremely skewed and required alternative analytical procedures that did not require assumptions of normality. We used a non-parametric bootstrap computer-intensive method to conduct power analyses with 2006 and 2007 data following methods outlined by Hamilton and Collings (1991). Ninety percent confidence intervals around means were calculated using the simple bootstrap percentile method described by Efron and Tibshirani (1993) and Manly (2001). Data from 0.5 m^2 quadrats in 2005 were scaled by 1.2 in order to make them comparable with 0.6 m^2 quadrats in subsequent years. We scaled all years by 1.66 in order to report estimates per m^2. We fit models of linear trend using ordinary least squares regression and non-parametric permutation methods to test the significance of and to estimate 90% confidence intervals around the regression slope coefficient β_1, following methods outlined by Manly (2001). Data were log transformed for this procedure, requiring interpretation of back-transformed estimates to be made in terms of a percent change in the median rather than the mean. Homogeneity of variances, an important assumption for ordinary least squares regression, was evaluated for each sampling frame (management zone) using the Fligner-Killeen test and the Bartlett test. According to these tests, log transformation was effective in establishing variance homogeneity in all frames except Weippe Prairie zone E. Only four years of data are available, trend estimates are imprecise and preliminary and should be interpreted with caution. Power to detect trends, if present, will increase with each subsequent year of sampling.

We summarized all four years of data graphically using a control or "conformance" chart approach following recommendations by Beauregard et al. (1992) and Morrison (2008). Because of our initial interest in "assessment points" $\pm$ 25% of a baseline mean value, the charts displayed here are a-statistical in the sense that control or "action" limits are not based on an underlying probability distribution but arbitrarily established at assessment point values. We used the mean of 2007 and 2008 mean values as a preliminary baseline, but note that baseline decisions will be updated as additional years of data become available. We conducted a fixed-effect meta-analysis of all 5 management zones for Weippe Prairie to provide an overall estimate of trend across the park unit for NEPE's annual resource stewardship summary reporting. This procedure provides a weighted average of reported effects (trend estimates, in this case) using the reciprocal of the variance for weights. No meta-analysis was required for BIHO reporting, as there is only one sampling frame. Finally, we evaluated the relationship between thatch depth and camas density using Kendall's τ correlation coefficient, a rank-based non-parametric approach to evaluating linear relationships between two variables. The correlation coefficient ranges from -1 to 1, and provides evidence of a negative relationship (large negative values), a positive relationship (large positive values), or absence of linear relationship (values near 0). All analyses and preparation for graphics were conducted in R software and computing environment (R version 2.7.2, http://www.r-project.org/).

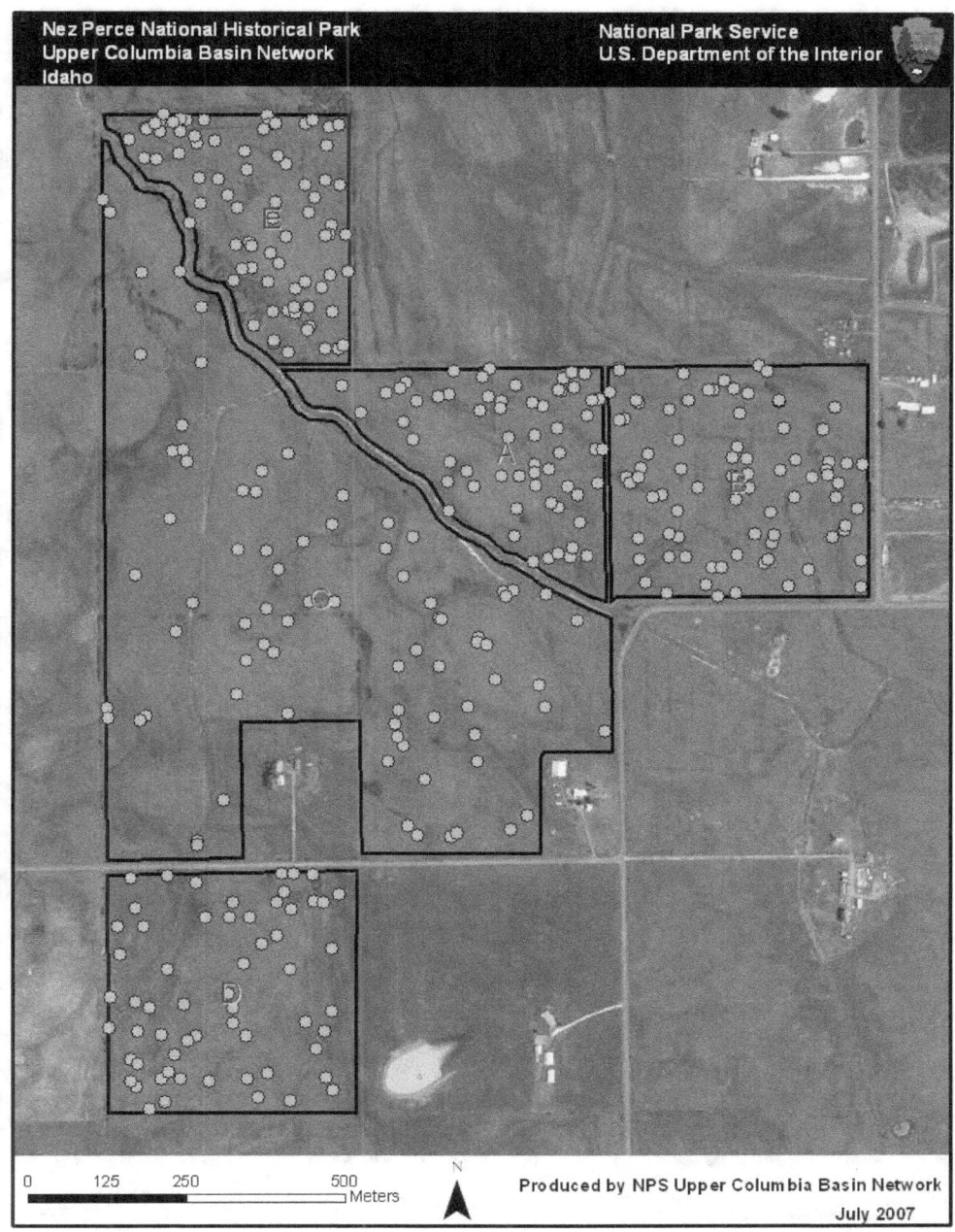

Figure 1. The camas monitoring sampling frame at Weippe Prairie, Nez Perce National Historical Park, including all 5 management zones (red letters A-E) and 2008 sampling locations (gray points). Details of sampling frame development are available in the UCBN camas monitoring protocol (Rodhouse et al. 2007).

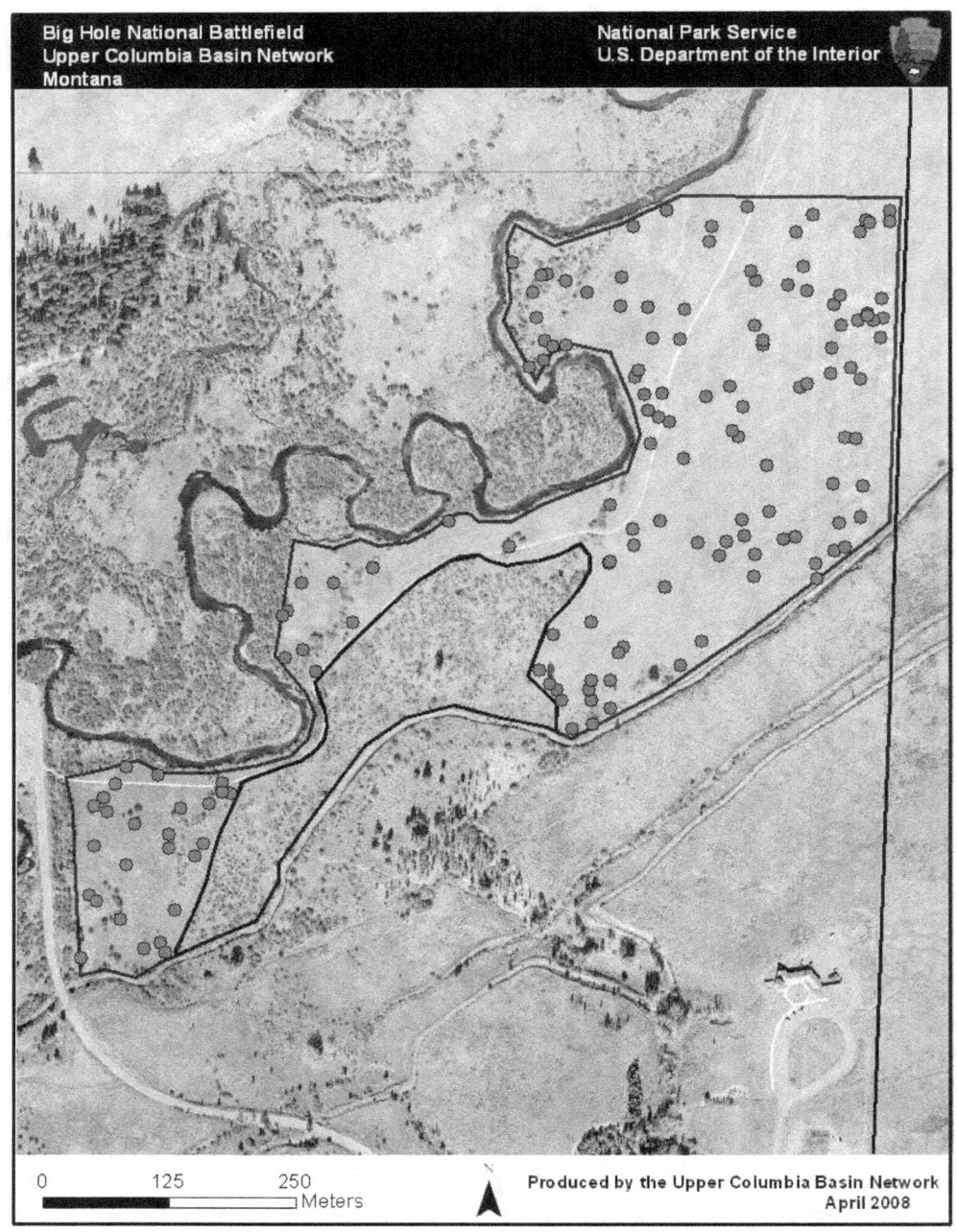

Figure 2. The camas monitoring sampling frame and 2008 sampling locations (gray points) at Big Hole National Battlefield. Details of the sampling frame and how boundaries were determined are available in the UCBN camas monitoring protocol (Rodhouse et al. 2007).

8

Results

Point estimates of means, confidence intervals, and flowering ratios for Weippe Prairie and BIHO are presented in Tables 1 and 2. Management zones A and D at Weippe Prairie were consistently the largest populations among the 6 sampling frames (including BIHO). Zone E was the smallest population, but these results may be biased low in 2006 and 2007 because of early livestock turnout into that area. Figure 3 presents control charts for each sampling frame. All populations fall within the conformance range during 2008 except zone E, which exhibited extreme fluctuations over the 4 year period. The baseline range for this population is not well characterized by the existing data. In 2006, evidence from zones B, C, D, and E suggests that densities were lower than subsequent years. This is striking given that a protocol change implemented in 2007 resulted in the counting of only "established" plants, and a drop between 2006 and 2007 counts was expected in the absence of a significant density increase. Flowering ratios were similar across all zones except for BIHO, which was considerably higher than Weippe Prairie ratios over 2007-2008. Note that the two largest populations, those of zones A and D, showed relatively stable flowering ratios over the three year period, whereas the zones with smaller populations had at least one marked change between years.

Table 3 presents preliminary trend estimates for each of the 6 populations. All zones showed a weak positive trend, but only zone C was statistically significant at the $\alpha=0.05$ level. Figure 4 presents the meta-analysis results for Weippe Prairie. The summary effect estimate for Weippe Prairie was 1.11 (i.e., an 11% annual rate of change in median density over all zones; 90% confidence interval 1.05-1.18). Note that the slope value 1.0 represents no trend for these back-transformed estimates, and confidence intervals include 1.0 (no trend or "0") for all zones except C.

Tables 4 and 5 present the estimates of current condition for the three camas vital sign measures for each management unit. These current condition estimates are the point estimates, rounded to the nearest integer, and are packaged for inclusion in park resource stewardship strategy reporting and vital signs summary tables.

The Kendall's τ correlation coefficient was $<|.2|$ for established density~thatch and flowering stem density~thatch across all zones and years, including BIHO, indicating no linear relationship between thatch depth and camas density. Figure 5 presents a scatterplot of 2008 density (log transformed) against thatch depth for zone C, graphically illustrating the lack of correlation observed across all management zones. Average thatch depths ranged from <1 cm to 3 cm, and appeared to vary randomly across years and zones. Figure 6 summarizes precipitation data for the Pierce, Idaho weather station for the 45-year period of record and for the years that precede and overlap sampling, beginning with 2004. Data from 2004 and 2005 show greater variability around the long-term average, with below average winter precipitation and above average spring precipitation. Precipitation during 2006-2008 was closer to the long-term average, with only one large positive deviation during fall 2006. The long-term average annual precipitation was 41 inches, and totals for the years 2004-2007 were 46, 37, 47, and 36 inches, respectively. Several more years of camas sampling is required before the effect of precipitation (and temperature) on camas populations can be evaluated. Finally, Table 6 presents weed frequencies and standard errors for each Weippe Prairie management zone for 2007 and 2008. Sulfur cinquefoil declines were observed in 2008 for all zones except E, and orange hawkweed declined slightly in zones A and D, and increased slightly in the other zones. Zones A and D have the lowest rates of invasion by these species overall.

Table 1. Means, 90% confidence intervals, and flowering ratios for Weippe Prairie camas populations, 2005-2008. Data are presented separately for each management zone. Confidence intervals were computed with the percentile bootstrap method outlined by Manly (2001).

Zone	Year	n	Plants/m^2 Density	90% percentile CI lower	upper	Plants/m^2 Flowers	90% percentile CI lower	upper	Flowering Ratio
A	2008	60	57.65	46.48	69.31	9.32	7.25	11.56	0.16
B	2008	80	7.14	4.13	10.54	1.22	0.64	1.97	0.17
C	2008	80	35.46	27.47	43.74	9.52	7.10	12.14	0.27
D	2008	60	56.94	37.02	79.18	9.43	6.45	12.81	0.17
E	2008	80	5.94	4.09	8.01	0.17	0.06	0.29	0.03
A	2007	65	61.65	48.96	74.93	7.81	6.00	9.76	0.13
B	2007	88	6.76	4.26	9.60	0.82	0.38	1.15	0.12
C	2007	60	29.63	20.28	39.92	6.03	3.90	8.52	0.20
D	2007	40	64.16	40.63	89.31	8.30	5.40	11.54	0.13
E	2007	30	0.44	0.11	0.83	0.17	0.06	0.33	0.37
A	2006	43	61.73	49.22	74.58	2.55	1.66	3.51	0.04
B	2006	17	2.64	0.39	5.27	0.68	0.00	1.46	0.26
C	2006	115	17.44	13.16	22.06	1.88	1.41	2.38	0.11
D	2006	30	33.31	17.76	51.68	3.65	2.05	5.42	0.11
E	2006	15	2.77	1.22	4.76	0.11	0.00	0.33	0.04
A	2005	25	48.67	32.93	65.87	NA	NA	NA	NA
B	2005	40	4.48	1.66	6.39	NA	NA	NA	NA
C	2005	87	20.78	14.18	28.07	NA	NA	NA	NA
D	2005	0	NA	NA	NA	NA	NA	NA	NA
E	2005	25	5.51	2.32	9.30	NA	NA	NA	NA

Table 2. Means, 90% confidence intervals, and flowering ratios for the BIHO camas population, 2006-2008. Confidence intervals were computed with the percentile bootstrap method outlined by Manly (2001).

Year	n	Plants/m^2 Density	90% CI lower	upper	Stems/m^2 Flowers	90% CI lower	upper	Flowering Ratio
2008	150	5.71	3.97	7.67	2.69	1.83	3.69	0.47
2007	124	3.86	2.53	5.52	1.90	1.25	2.68	0.49
2006	81	4.22	2.19	6.58	0.68	0.37	1.02	0.16

Table 3. Preliminary trend results for the period 2005-2008 using a randomization (permutation) approach to linear regression to assess the null hypothesis of no trend ($\beta_1=0$) over time in log-transformed camas density counts. Coefficients (for β_1) are back-transformed and should be interpreted as a multiplicative (percent) change in the median density of camas. For example, based on the observed data, zone C has undergone a 25% increase in the median number of established camas plants from 2005-2007. This trend was unlikely to have arisen by chance according to the permutation distribution used to calculate the p value. 90% confidence intervals, also back transformed, were computed using a randomization approach described by Manly (2001). These results are preliminary and should be interpreted with caution. Count data from 2005 and 2006 included seedlings as well as established plants. Variances for zone E were not homogeneous.

Zone	β_1(Year)	90%lower	90%upper	Direction	P
A	1.09	1.01	1.23	up	0.410
B	1.09	1.03	1.19	up	0.170
C	1.25	1.22	1.34	up	0.002
D	1.09	0.86	1.41	up	0.660
E	1.04	1.01	1.12	up	0.580
BIHO	1.10	0.99	1.20	up	0.148

Table 4. Vital sign summary information for the camas lily vital sign, Big Hole National Battlefield, 2008.

UCBN Vital Sign	Measure	Management Zone	Current Condition
Camas Lily			
Established stem density (established plants/m^2)		BIHO	6
Flowering stem density (flowering stems/m^2)		BIHO	3
Flowering ratio (flowering stems:established plants)		BIHO	0.47

Table 5. Vital sign summary information for the camas lily vital sign, Nez Perce National Historical Park, 2008.

UCBN Vital Sign	Measure	Management Zone	Current Condition
Camas Lily			
Established stem density (established plants/m^2)		Weippe Prairie A	58
		Weippe Prairie B	7
		Weippe Prairie C	35
		Weippe Prairie D	57
		Weippe Prairie E	6
Flowering stem density (flowering stems/m^2)		Weippe Prairie A	9
		Weippe Prairie B	1
		Weippe Prairie C	10
		Weippe Prairie D	9
		Weippe Prairie E	<1
Flowering ratio (flowering stems:established plants)		Weippe Prairie A	0.16
		Weippe Prairie B	0.17
		Weippe Prairie C	0.27
		Weippe Prairie D	0.17
		Weippe Prairie E	0.03
Orange hawkweed invasion (% frequency)		Weippe Prairie A	0
		Weippe Prairie B	5
		Weippe Prairie C	10
		Weippe Prairie D	2
		Weippe Prairie E	5
Sulphur cinquefoil invasion (% frequency)		Weippe Prairie A	3
		Weippe Prairie B	11
		Weippe Prairie C	5
		Weippe Prairie D	0
		Weippe Prairie E	8

Table 6. Weed frequency and standard errors (parentheses) for orange hawkweed (HIAU) and sulfur cinquefoil (PORE) for 2007 and 2008 at Weippe Prairie.

Zone	2008 HIAU	2008 PORE	2007 HIAU	2007 PORE
A	0.00(0.00)	0.03(0.23)	0.02(0.02)	0.09(0.04)
B	0.05(0.02)	0.11(0.04)	0.03(0.02)	0.20(0.04)
C	0.10(0.03)	0.05(0.02)	0.08(0.04)	0.18(0.05)
D	0.02(0.02)	0.00(0.00)	0.03(0.03)	0.00(0.00)
E	0.05(0.02)	0.08(0.03)	0.03(0.03)	0.07(0.07)

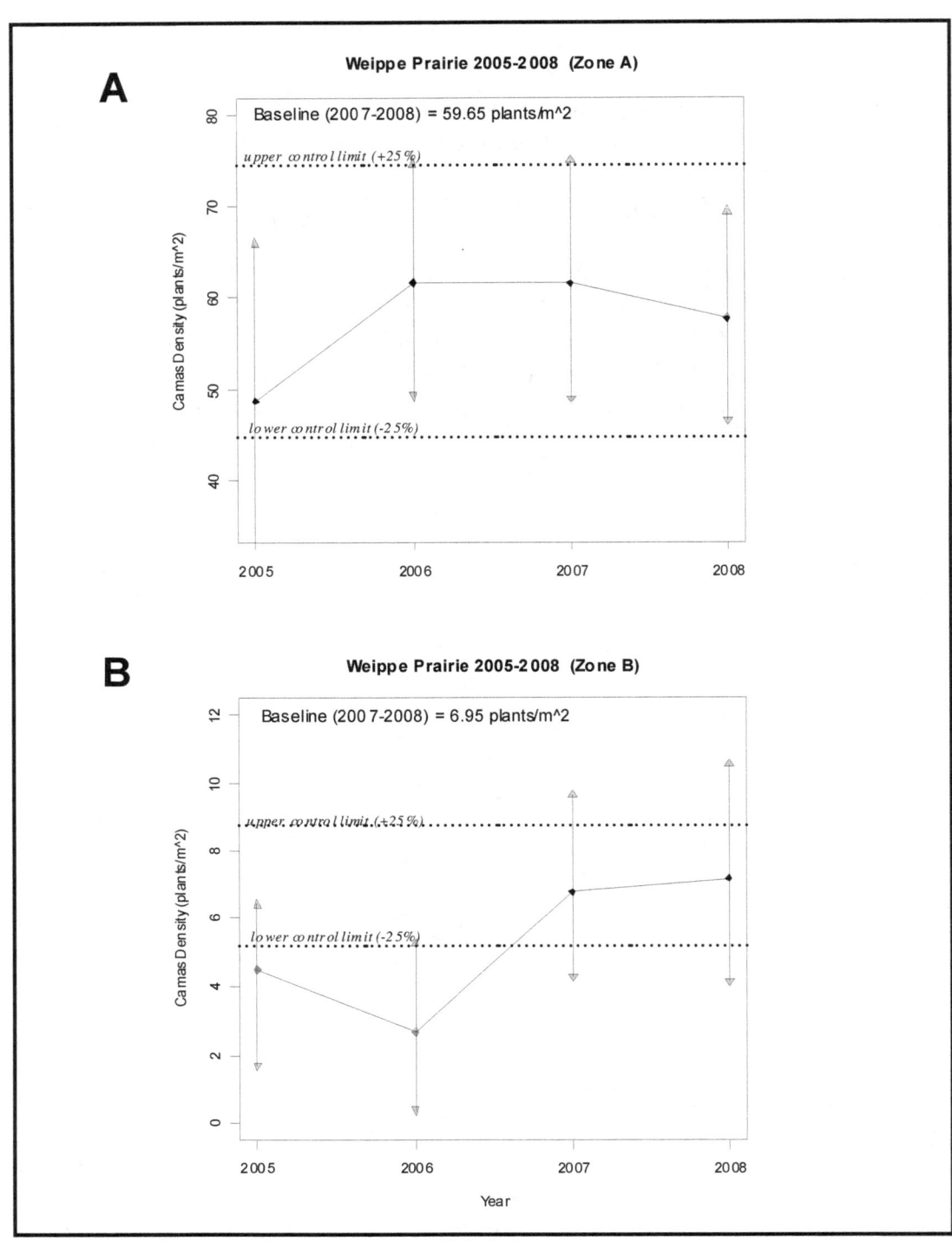

Figure 3. Control or "conformance" charts for each UCBN camas monitoring sampling frame for samples obtained during 2005-2008. Charts A-E illustrate respective Weippe Prairie management zones A-E. Chart F illustrates BIHO data. Means are center points with 90% confidence intervals as vertical arrows. Conformance bounds ($\bar{x} \pm 25\%$) are horizontal lines.

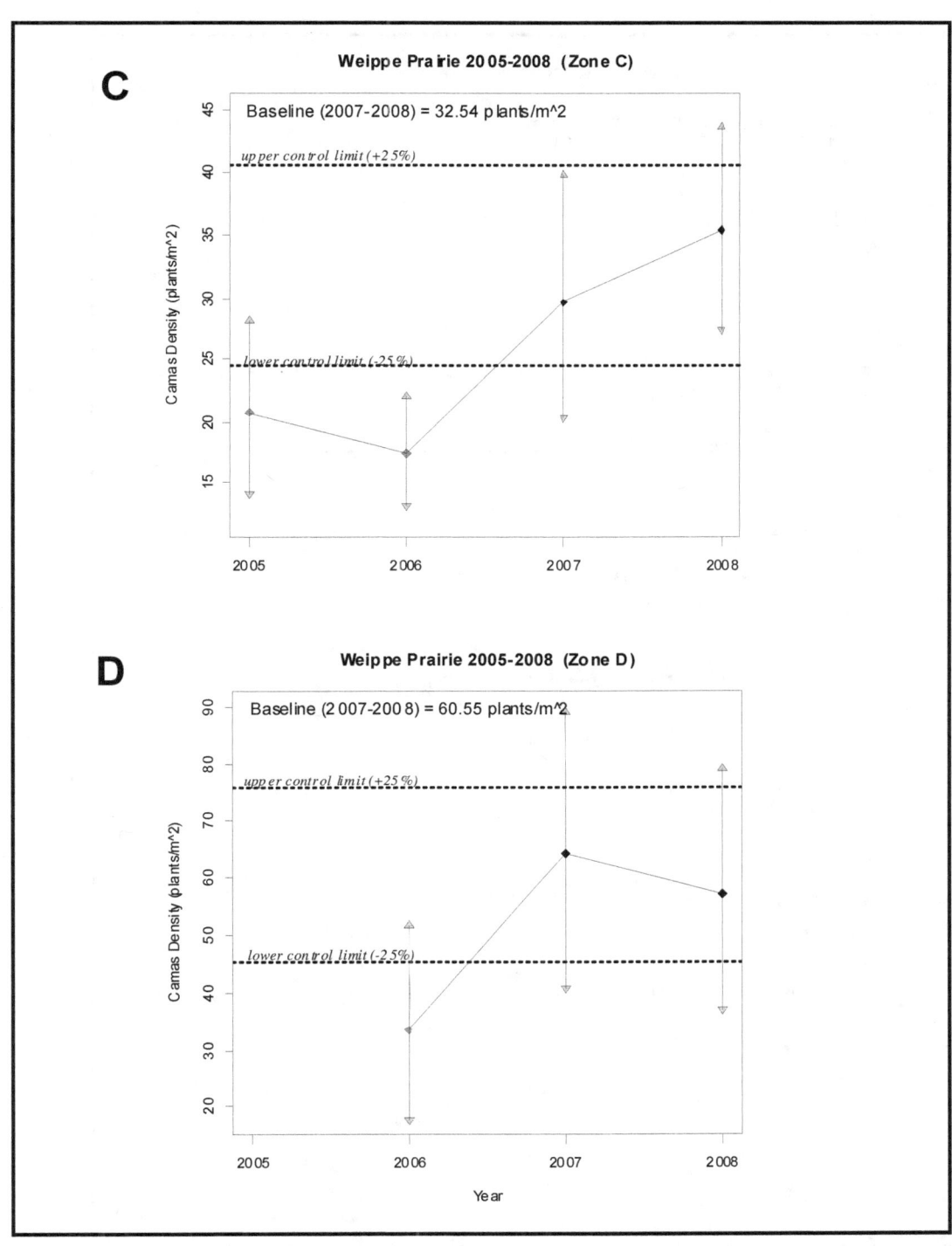

Figure 3. Control or "conformance" charts for each UCBN camas monitoring sampling frame for samples obtained during 2005-2008. Charts A-E illustrate respective Weippe Prairie management zones A-E. Chart F illustrates BIHO data. Means are center points with 90% confidence intervals as vertical arrows. Conformance bounds ($\bar{x} \pm 25\%$) are horizontal lines (continued).

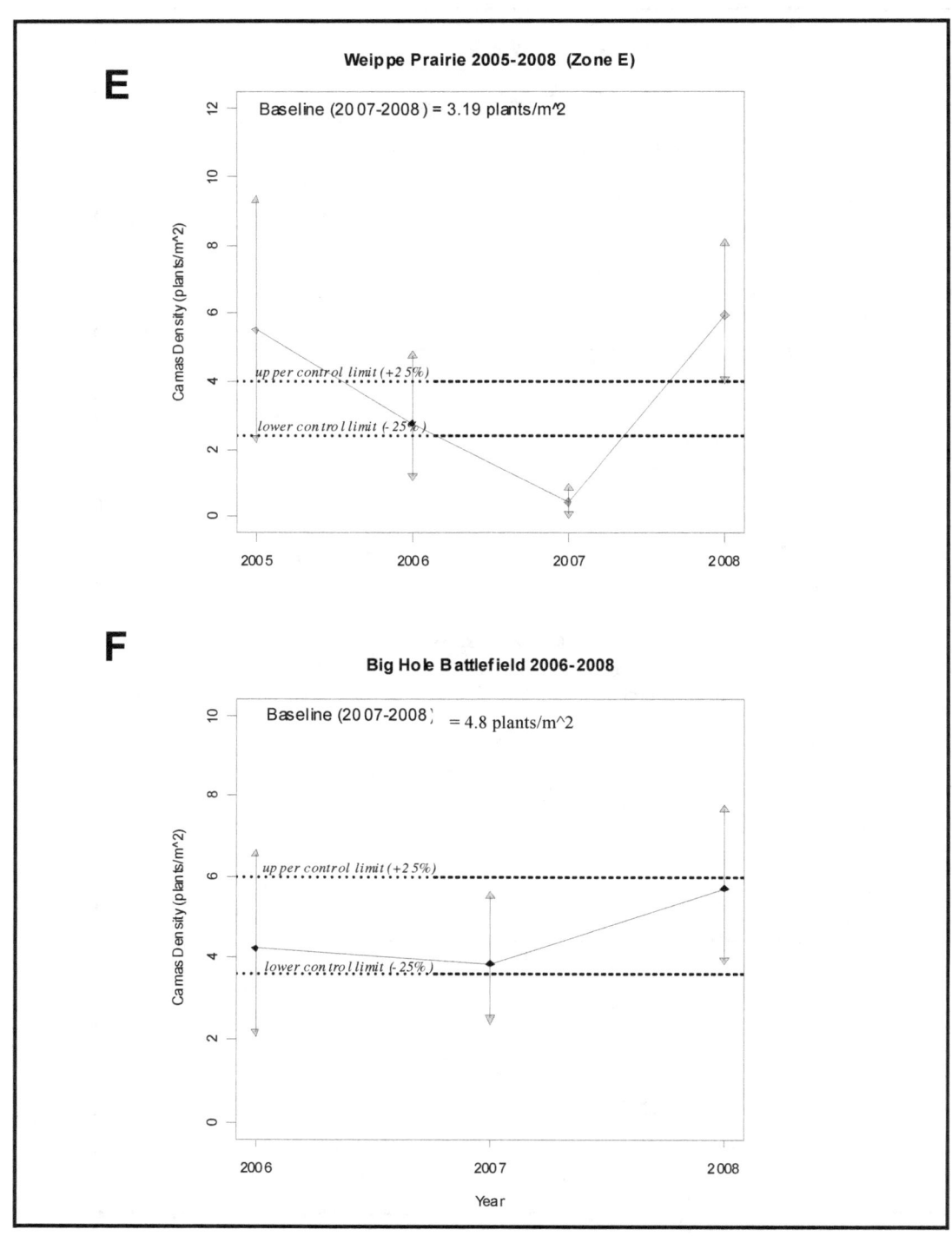

Figure 3. Control or "conformance" charts for each UCBN camas monitoring sampling frame for samples obtained during 2005-2008. Charts A-E illustrate respective Weippe Prairie management zones A-E. Chart F illustrates BIHO data. Means are center points with 90% confidence intervals as vertical arrows. Conformance bounds ($\bar{x} \pm 25\%$) are horizontal lines (continued).

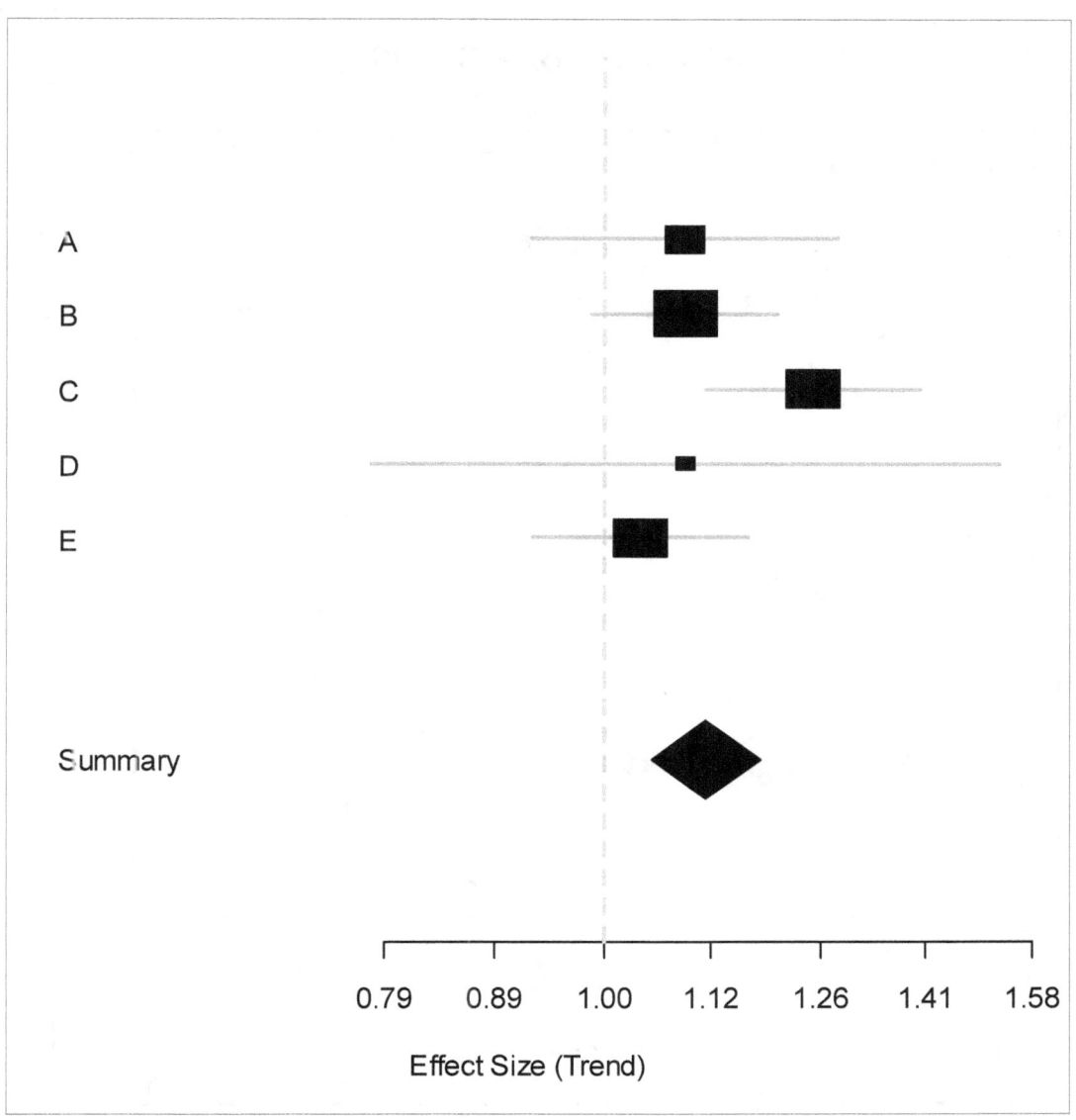

Figure 4. Meta-analysis plot for the estimates of trend in camas established plant density from each of the 5 Weippe Prairie management zones. The effect sizes (trend estimates) are back-transformed and represented in solid boxes scaled by the reciprocal of their variance. 90% confidence intervals are shown as horizontal lines. The estimated summary effect (1.11) is represented by the solid diamond. Note that the confidence intervals include 0 ($e^0=1$; no trend for all zones except C).

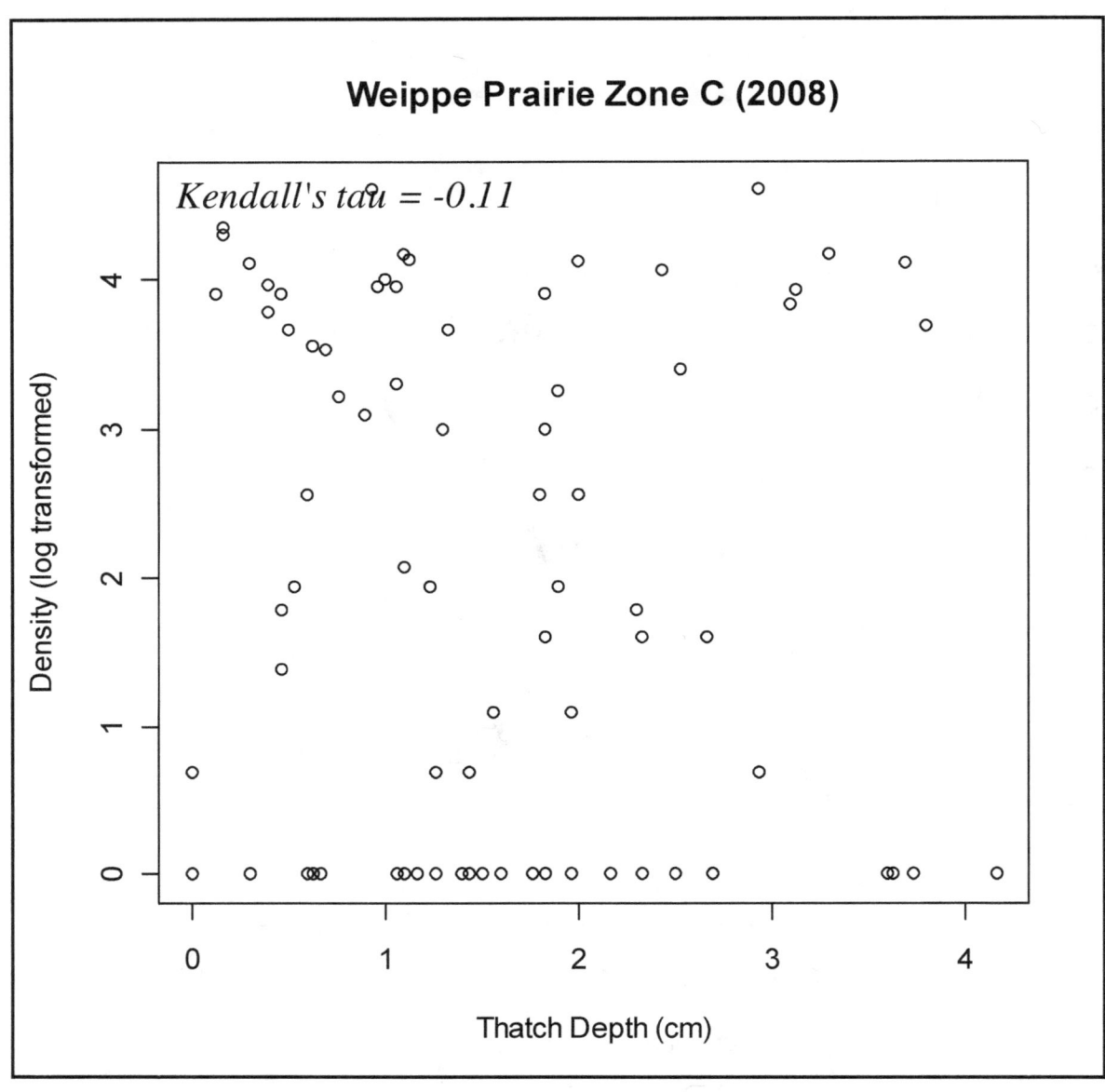

Figure 5. Scatterplot of 2008 established stem density counts (log transformed) versus thatch depth for Weippe Prairie management zone C. Kendall's tau was -0.11, suggesting no linear relationship between the two variables.

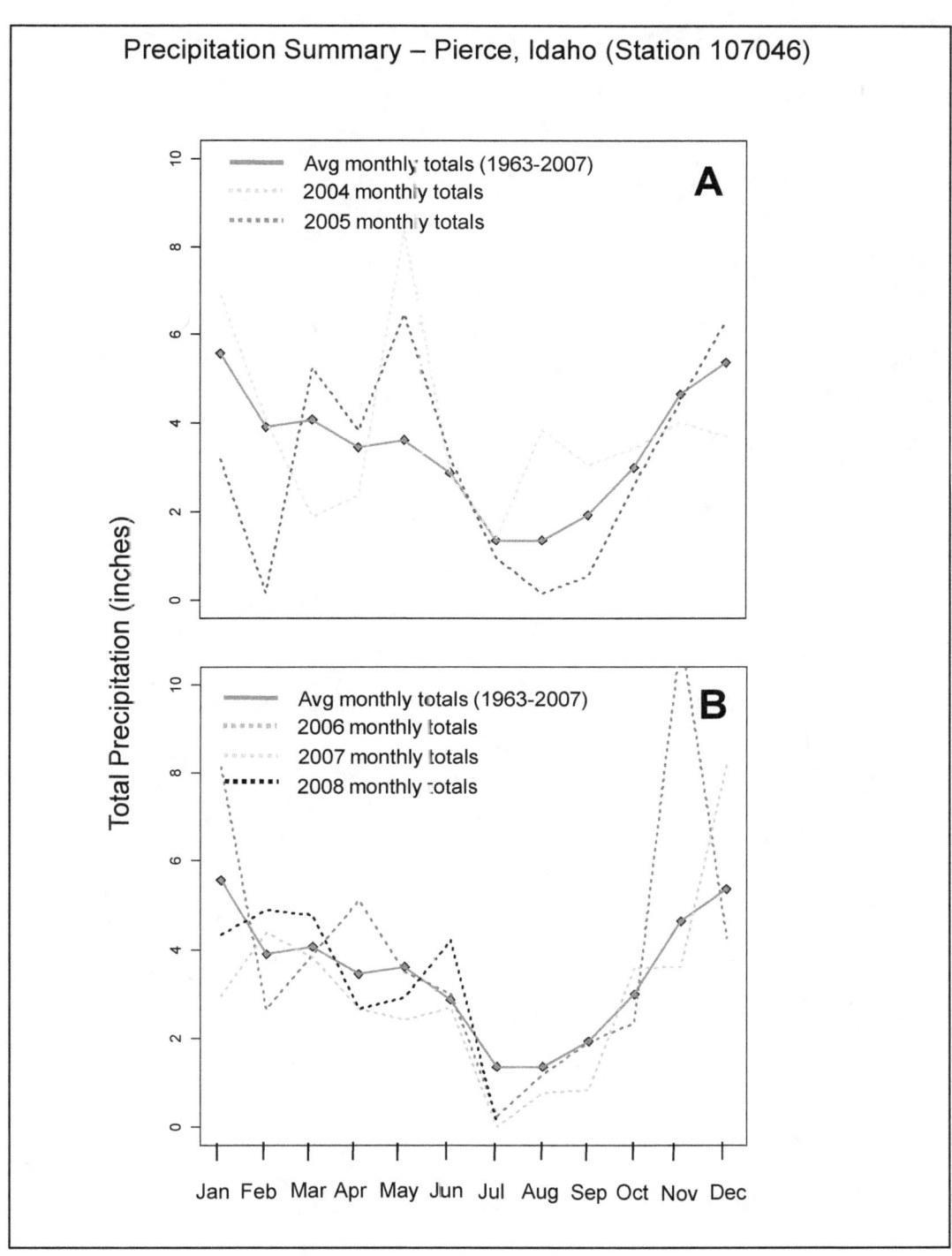

Figure 6. Mean monthly total precipitation (solid red) over the 45 year period of record 1963-2007, Pierce, Idaho, plotted with A) 2004 and 2005 and B) 2006-2008 monthly totals.

Discussion

The UCBN camas monitoring program has begun to characterize both the baseline central tendency of camas abundance as well as the variability in that abundance across six NPS management zones in two parks, NEPE and BIHO. Each of these zones appear to have unique populations (in terms of location and scale), and they are being treated independently for analytical and reporting purposes. These zones represent a broad range in overall density and in flowering ratios. Zones A and D at Weippe Prairie have the largest populations, with approximately 60 plants/m^2, although these are still below historic estimates available from the ethnobotanical and archaeological literature (Thoms 1989). Zone E has the smallest population, and was most heavily impacted by permitted grazing during the start-up years of monitoring. The increase in zone E density in 2008 is promising, although we underscore our reluctance to ascribe any relationship between cessation of grazing and increasing density. Sampling error resulting from a simple inability to see plant leaves clipped down by livestock during sampling may explain this pattern more than any real change in the population size. However, we note that there appears to be an overall trend among all six zones of stable to increasing populations, the lack of statistical significance in these trends notwithstanding (e.g., Figure 4). The increase in density after 2006 (Zone E excepted) is striking given the protocol change initiated after 2006 sampling in which only "established" camas plants were included in density counts. This change was expected to result in a sharp decrease in density counts in 2007.

There was no apparent relationship between thatch depth and established plant and flowering stem densities in any of the management zones, despite suggestions of such a relationship made in the context of traditional management practices involving burning and increased camas productivity (Storm and Shebitz 2006). Cessation of thatch depth measurements would reduce field time considerably in the future. We recommend suspending the collection of thatch depth in all zones except zone C. This zone has a relatively small sample size (n=60), and includes a range of camas density conditions.

Graphical exploration of precipitation patterns during the period of study provides no clear evidence of a relationship with camas density or flowering. However, there is considerable variability in both precipitation and density, and any relationship will require additional years of sampling before becoming apparent. Also, temperature may be important, and may interact with precipitation and site hydrology in complex ways to influence available soil moisture during critical periods such as spring germination. A study of soil moisture patterns has been initiated at Weippe Prairie by University of Idaho collaborators and will shed light on this important question. Light detection and ranging (laser altimetry or "LiDAR") information will be collected at Weippe Prairie in fall 2008, providing high resolution topographical data for modeling of camas density and flowering patterns.

Finally, frequencies of the two target weeds at Weippe Prairie are remaining stable or decreasing slightly. This is significant because Weippe Prairie was only acquired by NPS in 2003 and the potential for dramatic weed invasion accompanying land use changes associated with ownership was of concern to park managers. It is noteworthy that the two zones of highest camas density, A and D, appear to have the lowest rates of invasion.

Literature Cited

Angiosperm Phylogeny Group (APG). 2003. An update of the Angiosperm Phylogeny Group classification for the orders and families of flowering plants: APG II. Botanical Journal of the Linnaean Society **141**:399-436.

Bennetts, R. E., J. E. Gross, K. Cahill, C. McIntyre, B. B. Bingham, A. Hubbard, L. Cameron, and S. L. Carter. 2007. Linking monitoring to management and planning: assessment points as a generalized approach. George Wright Forum **24**:59-77.

Beauregard, M. R., R. J. Mikulak, and B. A. Olson. 1992. A practical guide to statistical quality improvement: opening up the statistical toolbox. Van Nostrand Reinhold, New York.

Dahl, T. E. 1990. Wetlands: losses in the United States: 1780's to 1980's. US Fish and Wildlife Service, Washington DC.

Efron, B., and R. Tibshirani. 1993. An introduction to the bootstrap. Chapman and Hall, London.

Gould, F. W. 1942. A systematic treatment of the genus *Camassia* Lindl. American Midland Naturalist **28**:712-742.

Hamilton, M. A., and B. J. Collings. 1991. Determining the appropriate sample size for nonparametric tests for location shift. Technometrics **33**:327-337.

Harbinger L. J. 1964. The importance of food plants in the maintenance of Nez Perce cultural identity. Thesis. Washington State University, Pullman, WA.

Havard, V. 1895. Food plants of the American Indians. Bulletin of the Torrey Botanical Club **22**:98-123.

Hunn E. S. 1981. On the relative contribution of men and women to subsistence among hunter-gathers of the Columbia Plateau: a comparison with *Ethnographic Atlas* summaries. Journal of Ethnobiology **1**:124-134.

Leiberg, J. B. 1897. General report on a botanical survey of the Coeur d'Alene mountains in Idaho. Contributions of the U.S. National Herbarium. Vol V., No. 1., Washington DC.

MacDonald, T. 2003. Review of environmental monitoring methods: survey designs. Environmental Monitoring and Review **85**:277-292.

Manly, B. F. J. 2001. Randomization, Bootstrap and Monte Carlo Methods in Biology. Chapman and Hall/CRC, Boca Raton, FL.

Mastrogiuseppe, J. 2000. Nez Perce ethnobotany: a synthetic review. Report to Nez Perce National Historic Park, Spalding, ID. Project # PX9370-97-024.

Meehan, T. 1898. The plants of Lewis and Clark's expedition across the continent, 1804-1806. Proceedings of the Academy of Natural Sciences of Philadelphia **50**:12-49.

Morrison, L. 2008. The use of control charts to interpret monitoring data. Natural Areas Journal **28**:66-73.

Murphey, E. V. A. 1987. Indian Uses of Native Plants. Mendocino County Historical Society, Ukiah, CA.

Reed, P. B., Jr. 1988. National list of plant species that occur in wetlands: 1988 national summary. U.S. Fish and Wildlife Service. Biological Report **88** (24).

Rodhouse, T. J., M. V. Wilson, K. M. Irvine, R. K. Steinhorst, G. H. Dicus, L. K. Garrett, and J. W. Lyon. 2007. Camas lily monitoring protocol. Version 1.0. Natural Resource Report NPS/UCBN/NRR—2007/011. National Park Service, Fort Collins, Colorado.

Storm, L., and D. Shebitz. 2006. Evaluating the purpose, extent, and ecological restoration applications of indigenous burning practices of southwestern Washington. Ecological Restoration **24**:256-268.

Taft, O. W., and S. M. Haig. 2003. Historical wetlands in Oregon's Willamette Valley: implications for restoration of winter waterbird habitat. Wetlands **23**:51-64.

Thoms, A. 1989. The northern roots of hunter-gatherer intensification: camas and the Pacific Northwest. Dissertation. Washington State University, Pullman, WA.

Turner, N. J., and H. V. Kuhnlein. 1983. Camas (*Camassia* spp.) and riceroot (*Fritillaria* spp.): two liliaceous "root" foods of the Northwest Coast Indians. Ecology of Food and Nutrition **13**:199-219.

NPS/UCBN/NRTR-2008/133